LOOK DEEPLY

LOOK DEEPLY

Prayers and photographs by Charles D. Robison

JUDSON PRESS
Valley Forge

Dedicated to the good people
of Huntington, West Virginia,
who helped us make our first home,
taught us their wisdom,
suffered through many a boring sermon,
and held still for many snapshots.

Our Father, when we look out on these old hills that protect us from everything but ourselves, we are easily reminded that Your love is just as old, just as unchanging, just as strong as these hills.

We thank You that Your creation sustains us and renews our own lives, even as our world is renewed.

We thank You for the wisdom that one generation passes on to the next.

And we thank You for little children
who can disarm us with their smiles,
and pain us with their tears.

We thank You for other people who share our lives with us and help us to see beyond ourselves.

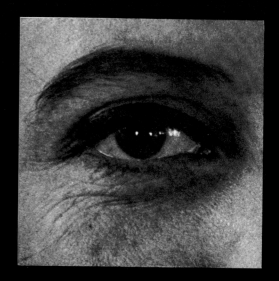

We thank You that each of us has problems and joys that we can share with those close to us. We thank You that we have been given the freedom to look deeply into life. And we thank You that when we do look, we are able to see a Christ who came to increase our freedom and to reveal Your ways to man.

We thank You for families and friends—
and even for the folks we don't like,
because they remind us of our own short-
comings.

You have given us Your Son to believe in, to trust in, to hope in, and to die and be raised from the dead in. We are thankful—

For our brothers whom we can so easily
ignore by calling them welfare cases,
or bums, or loafers.

For the poor in the streets—and in the slums—who watch our luxuries on television with one eye, and see rats running across their floors with the other.

For our brothers whom we can lock away in dungeons because their minds don't work like ours do.

For our brothers whom we can consider as lesser animals by calling them niggers . . .

For the lucky and the prosperous
that they might find the real victory
of their accomplishment in humble
sharing with others.

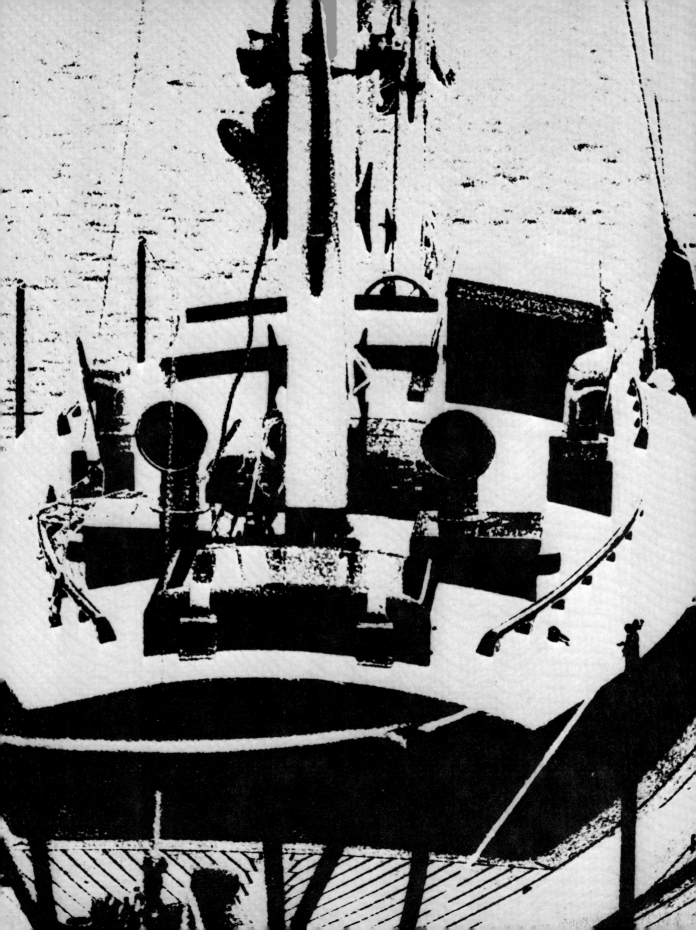

We pray for our friends who have lost a person they loved. Keep Your promise of eternal life as close to their hearts as the tears are to their eyes.

Teach us to pray, Father, not with memorized words and phrases, but with our hands and minds and hearts. Give us the conviction to bridge the credibility gap between what we confess to believe and what we actually do with our lives.

There are mothers who will watch us parade our Easter finery to church— and hate themselves because their children still don't have shoes.

Father, we remember what it felt like when, as little children, we got lost from our parents in a crowd. How alone and frightened and scared we were, and we know that too many people feel this way too often today. Make us sensitive to them. Teach us to communicate.

And when the loneliness of our own lives becomes almost unbearable, help us not to forget the tragedy in the lives of others—

The tragedy of being old in a world taking
its lead from the Pepsi Generation.

The tragedy of our mental hospitals—
where we corral people until they die,
which makes us content to be our brother's
keeper, rather than our brother's brother.

We want to pray for the people who are sick and in pain. We want them to get well, to come outside again and play like little children. It makes us angry —sometimes at You—when we learn that some of them will never come outside again, that some of them are waiting now to die.

Give us the wisdom to see need, even when
it is clothed in the garments of
self-sufficiency.

Our Father we pray, and we wonder if You really hear, and then we wonder if we are really praying. And we want to pray, and we want You to listen, and we want to know, somehow, that You do listen.

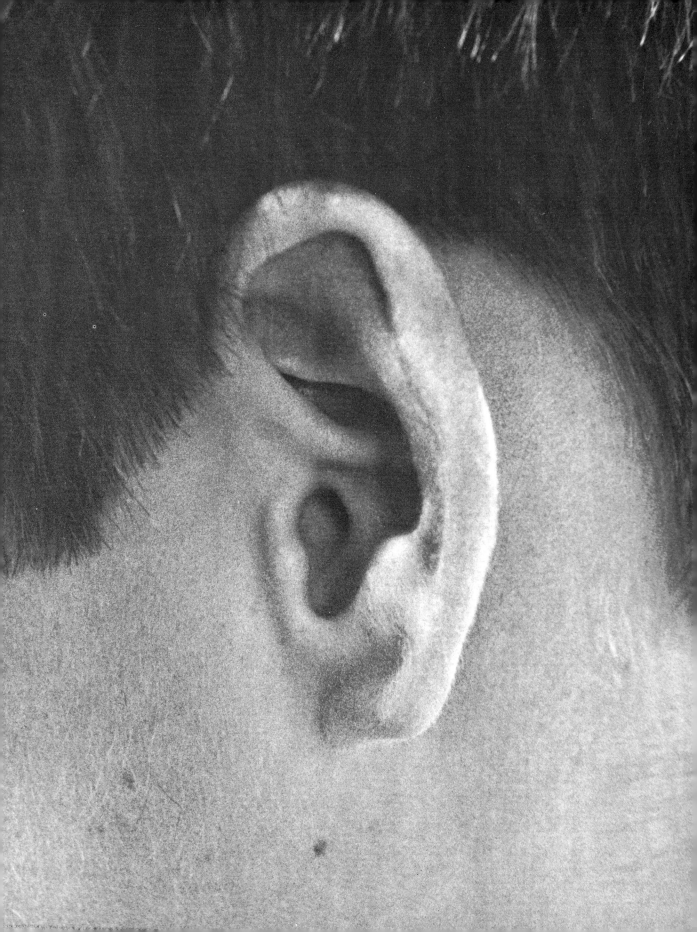

We have said that we love our neighbor as
much as ourselves, but the truth is that
we are killing our neighbors, not so
much with the things that we do as with
the things that we do not do. We have
not been patient with our brothers. We
have turned aside when our brothers have
not been quick to adopt our ways, our values,
our standards. And we have not let our
brothers be as free as we like to think
we are.

Help us to help the old . . . with respect
. . . with appreciation for what their labors
have given us.

Our Father and our God, the withered lives
we bring to You for forgiveness are not
what we wish, or what You have directed.

When we can no longer hide our guilt from ourselves, we fumble with the invisible beads of our religion until the pain eases off and we go again our own ways.

RIDE
CLOUD NINE
AND THE
HAUNTED HOUSE
WELCOME

Our trouble is that we are afraid to
pray. We try so often, and so often we
feel like we are not using the right
words, or concentrating hard enough.
And sometimes we feel like our prayers
are never heard. Help us to pray, Father.
Help us to remember that our most important
prayers are not made up of words, but of
tears and laughter. And keep us from being
beggars when we pray, asking for those
things which we neither need nor intend
to use.

Also we have forgotten who we are. Instead of seeing ourselves as Your children, saved through the death of Your own Son, we have been content to think of ourselves as Americans, white people, Protestants, middle-class people. Father, teach us patience, give us the will to care for other people, and help us to see ourselves for what we really are—even Your children.

Our Father, we have been trampling in
Your vineyards. We have told ourselves
we were doing Your labor, but we now know
that the grapes of Your wrath are stored
there for us—who deserve not only
Your wrath, but to be banished from
Your sight.

We grow secure in our ability to not hear Your knock at the doors of our lives. When we haven't told lies about other people, we have been content to let lies be told without challenge.

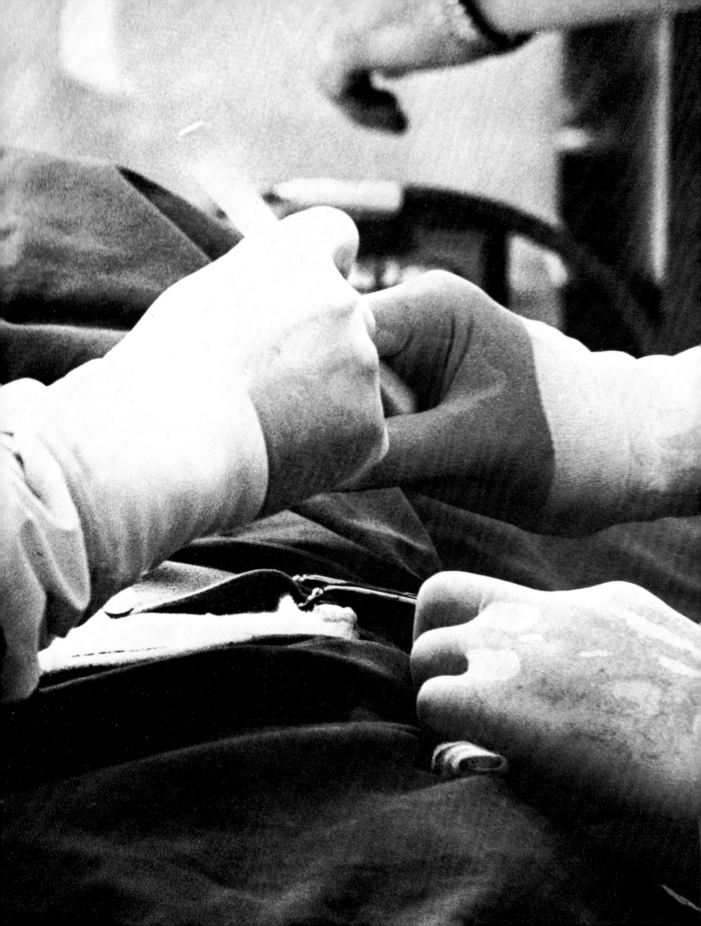

If prayer is where we are to start, help us to forget our concerns for saying the right words, and set us to praying with our hands and with our hearts—

For our brothers who have black skin, empty pockets, and who speak a different language than we do.

For our brothers who are old and tired and lonely—who have sent all their friends back to dust.

For those who feel lost—lost from
other men, and from any kind of relation-
ship with You—help them find the way
from those who are sure.

For the people who live in ghettoes—
the white ghettoes and the black ghettoes
alike—let there be an understanding com-
munication.

Take the words of peace and plant them in
the hearts of the leaders of men.

Match our fear of involvement with an
equally strong consciousness of the
growth that only comes from involvement.

We have not sought the truth, but rather have been content with rumors and hints of rumors.

Help us to care for the needy. We see
them every day—at work, at school,
in the streets. We see so much of them
that we become numb to their plight, and
our numbness gives way to excuses for
not being able to care. And our own
very pressing needs keep us from
sacrificing the extra amount they need.
Dear God, help us to trust in You for
our needs, so that we can give ourselves
to the needs of others.

And we thank You for little children, who crawl and then walk, who know the spontaneity of laughter and tears, who remind us that we will have to become like them if we are to enter the kingdom of heaven.

As we are newly aware of our status as children before You, make us shockingly aware that all men are our brothers, members of one family, headed all in one direction—home to You.

Help us to not use Your name in vain—
by calling on You with words of thanks-
giving, but failing to live like we are
truly thankful and truly concerned.

Do for us what we cannot do for ourselves.
Lead us into a new tomorrow with a new
spirit. Cleanse our hearts and create within
us new attitudes and new ideas, as only
You can create them.

We make bold to say: Our heavenly Father,
may we realize Your greatness, and as we
become more and more aware of it, may our
lives be Yours and reflect Your love. We
know we cannot live without You, for without food from Your earth our bodies starve,
and without Your presence our spirits wither.
Forgive us, as we know we hurt You: and we, forgiven,
can forgive those who hurt us. Keep us strong
during our testing that we may not be evil.
The universe is Yours, as is the reason and
glory of life. Amen.